THE ELEPHANT & THE GORILLA

THE ELEPHANT
& THE GORILLA
and Other Stories by African Children

First published 2015

Country Setting
www.countrysetting.co.uk

©Veronica Leach
On behalf of the Coloma School, Uganda, 2015

Veronica Leach has asserted her rights under
the Copyright, Designs and Patents Act 1988
to be identified as the author of this work

All rights reserved. No part of this publication may be reproduced
or transmitted in any form or by any means, electronic or mechanical,
including photocopying, recording, or any information storage or
retrieval system, without prior permission in writing from the publishers.

Pictures reproduced by kind permission of ©Veronica Leach

Cover design by Anna Trussler using original illustrations
by children from Coloma Primary School

British Library Cataloguing-in-Publication Data

A catalogue record for this book is available from the British Library

ISBN: PB: 978-0-9559998-2-6

Typeset by Country Setting, Kingsdown, Kent CT14 8ES

Printed and bound in Great Britain by BookEmpire, UK

THE ELEPHANT & THE GORILLA

and Other Stories by African Children

Selected by
Veronica Leach

With support from the
Ronald Duncan Literary Foundation

Dedication

In gratitude to all those who have listened to our children,
and in so doing gave them a voice.
And for all the 'Little Voices' as yet unheard.

Learning for Life provides education, food, healthcare and support for many traumatised and needy children and young people in Uganda

Coloma Primary School provides life changing care and education for children in need in Uganda. The Coloma Teachers inspired and made this book possible

The Ronald Duncan Literary Foundation exists to encourage and support creative excellence in the arts, especially poetry, drama and literature and to sustain interest and research in the work associated with its namesake, the poet and playwright, Ronald Duncan. Duncan's archive is now housed at the University of Exeter as part of their Special Collections of South West based writers. www.ronaldduncanfoundation.co.uk

Preface

In an age of technology, children and young people in the so-called developed world have much to say, emboldened by a culture of self-expression: social media, smart phones and tweets. It is almost unimaginable that in many parts of our now very-small world, there are so many children whose voices remain unheard.

In the course of my work with vulnerable children and young people in Uganda, I have had the privilege of hearing the stories of children whose lives are devoid of educational opportunity. The children I work with have experienced abuse in many forms: exploitation, trauma, hunger, poverty and disease.

Many of these children are alone, orphaned, abandoned or else trafficked, and must resort to any means available for their survival.

Were you to drive through the congestion and chaos of Kampala you would see children, often with babies on their backs, begging. In spite of such deprivation, they live in the hope of a chance to learn.

My wish is to provide the means of shelter, clothing, education and support for children and young people in Uganda. Due to the generosity of people in the UK, much has already been achieved. Many have been educated and are now able to provide not only for themselves but for their siblings, while some are still in school or college, in the knowledge that education is the key to a better life.

Sadly, some of the children are unable to learn or develop at school, traumatised by their past experiences. A large part of my work is to help them to realise their potential. To tell their stories. To express what is shut away, and to be heard. This is a very personal and private sharing.

In 2013, I was invited to apply to the Ronald Duncan Literary Foundation for funding to promote an essay-writing competition at Coloma Primary School. The pupils attending Coloma come from all over Uganda, The Democratic Republic of Congo and Rwanda. The Trust provided notebooks, writing materials and prizes of dictionaries and books for this enterprise. My challenge then was to encourage 64 children to write an essay entitled, "My Life".

Coming from a society where oral traditions still predominate, the children invited to participate had no previous experience of essay-writing or comprehension. Undaunted, during the next three days, they embraced this challenge enthusiastically, despite their demanding school timetable. Dictionaries aside, the children received no other assistance or direction from either their English teachers, or me.

The Trustees were so moved by the efforts of the pupils and the stories they told, that the Foundation agreed to give them the opportunity to share their experiences with a wider audience by publishing some of the entries. There is little, if any, published children's literature originating in Uganda, and we felt that seeing their work in print might encourage and inspire these young authors.

We have chosen forty-one of the original sixty-four essays which include personal narratives, traditional folklore and fiction. We hope that this selection of essays will amuse and inform you, and provide an insight into the lives of a small group of African children, representing so many others who long to have a voice and to be heard.

The children and I are indebted to those whose support has made this book possible.

Veronica Leach

CONTENTS OF STORIES

PART ONE: My Life, My Story

1.	The Woman Who Had a Tail	Ella	2
2.	My Mother Survived Rwanda	Claire	4
3.	My Hair Gives Me Knowledge	Doreen	6
4.	A Bag Full of Rabbit	Patience	8
5.	The Journey	Eileen	9
6.	Violence Remembered	Lynn	10
7.	The Boy Who Knocked Me Down	Esme	11
8.	Hunger	Helen	12
9.	Reward For a Monkey Restored	Hope	14
10.	The Day My Father Died	Content	17
11.	My Trip to the Lake	Celia	18
12.	My Hair	Mona	19

PART TWO: A Tale I Was Told

13.	Everybody Has The Right to a Name	Petal	22
14.	Is God in America?	Charity	24
15.	The Big Animal Who Taught Manners	Kitty	25
16.	Itching	Prudence	26
17.	The Green Snake	Mary	27
18.	A Christmas Tale	Sacha	28
19.	Boo Learns a Lesson	Denise	28
20.	Pots	Fern	29
21.	The Sack	Cynthia	30

22.	The Story of Lule	Patrica	32
23.	Bad Behaviour	Nita	32
24.	Snake Bite	Maria	33
25.	Uganda at War	Kuna	34
26.	The Witch Doctor	Peace	37
27.	Mr. Hare	Bani	38
28.	The Right Decision	Regina	39
29.	The Broken Cup	Tina	40
30.	The Slave	Sophie	42
31.	The Elephant and the Gorilla	Desire	42
32.	Kanyeyite – The Old Man	Anna	43
33.	Jane and Joan	Vic	44
34.	Legs	Andrew	46
35.	The Man Who Ate His Eye	Sarah	49
36.	The Sad King	Esther	52
37.	Sisters - How to Behave	Pia	54
38.	Chris Finds a Baby	Vita	56
39.	How to Behave – A Lesson	Petra	58
40.	The Girl Who Sang	Mercy	60
41.	The Greedy Man	Liz	62

NOTE: The children's use of "Ugandan" English has not been changed in the transcribed stories, in order to preserve their vernacular.

PART ONE:
My Life, My Story

1. The Woman Who Had a Tail

MY LIFE

When I was two years old, there was a storm. When the storm stopped, I went out to see how the enviroment looked like. When I was looking, I saw a naked woman with a tail. I was scared and ran inside the house and talked to the woman for a while.

They entered the house, gave her clothes and food. That night, I was scared to sleep. I wondered how an old woman could sit nakedly in the compound. I wondered all these things because I did not know where the woman came from. But my parents knew. While I was still wondery, I fell asleep and the night went by.

My mother was six months pregnant. We cared for the woman and she was soon fat and beautiful. We nicknamed her "share" but her name was "Carlita". One day when her and I were going to the markets she was seen by a man who admired her. The next day, the man came to ask for her hand in marriage and they allowed him. After her marriage, she was taken, and told the man that in their custom, they would not allow a man to touch the buttocks of a woman

The man telling the woman never to touch her buttocks.

At home they lived with the mother of the man. The woman is the one who mingled millet. One day when I was passing by, I saw a terrible thing. The woman was mingling millet with her tail. I watched her for a long time and when the millet was ready, I ran and sat in house. That day I did not eat. The same thing happened the next day. They asked me why I did not eat. I told the mother of the man. She did not believe me until she saw for herself. She could not wait to anounce it at lunch.

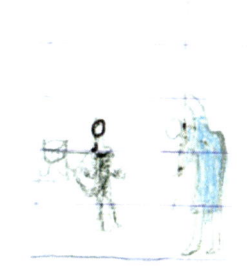

They were abusive to the woman. When the storm came, the woman disappeared with one child. In the morning the man searched for his wife. He had the news that the woman had gone where she came from. The storm came and the man disappeared. After all these problems my parents came and took me home. They told me that the man came back with the wife and lived happily.

END BY ELLA

2. My Mother Survived – Rwanda

MY LIFE.

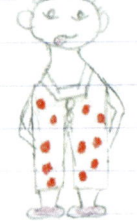

I am thirteen years old.
When I was ten years old, my mother told me her life story in the Genocide, which took place in Rwanda. It was led by the "Genius" who were the Bahutu to the Batutsi in April 1994.

THIS IS THE STORY.

APRIL 1994.

It was one day in Rwanda, when the Genocide begun. The Bahutu were against the Batutsi. In the areas of Rwanda there was sorrow, people were seeing their relatives being killed, children see their parents and sisters being killed, so it was very bad.

A family where my mother comes from, was visited by a friend. My grandmother told stories to that visitor, then it was time for the visitor to leave my grandmothers home. My grandmother escorted her peacefully. On her way back home after escorting the visitor, she was shot to death by the "Genius".

After a short time, my grandfather went to look for her and he was also shot to death. But my mother, her sisters, brothers and a child who had visited them did not know what was taking place at the time.

It was the night when the "Genius" started shooting in the sky to alert the people. The people were scattered, my mother and her brother went their own way and the other of her three sisters, two brothers and a child who had visited them went their own way. One of her sisters who had got married, had a baby boy on her back. A "Genius" who was a child himself came to her and took her hand, he shouted to the other "Genius" who were far from him saying, here is a Mututsi! Come all of you. My aunt said to him with a lot of anger and power, " you stupid boy, leave my hand", and she went to where the good soldiers were helping rescued people, to give them protection.

My mother and her brother were talking about which one of them should go to see the other sisters and brothers. They agreed together and went to find their sisters and brothers. As they were still going on, they were caught by the "Genius". The "Genius" took them to where they were beating the other children and that's where they saw their sisters and brothers being beaten. Because they were still young the "Genius" never beat them, but there was a "Genius" who knew them, and told other "Genius" to forgive them. They went each on her and his way.

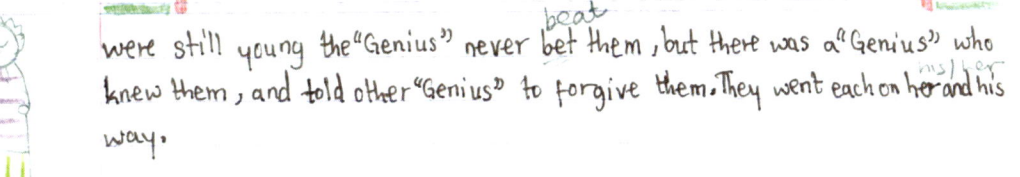

It was at night when my mother was still looking where to hide, she saw a house nearby where she went to ask for where to sleep during one night. The people in that house made my mother to sleep in the outside room which had no windows and doors. It was just a room. When the birds started singing early in the morning, my mother ran away from that house because she thought that she would be killed by the "Genius". She went to another house where she found a woman sweeping the compound. My mother asked her if she would help her with where to sleep for only one day, but that woman told my mother to hurry and get away because her husband was soon coming back to his home, and if he would find my mother there he would easily kill her, and kill his wife because of bringing the Mututsi in his home.

After that, my mother reached the place where she found some good soldiers who protected survivors. They gave my mother some water to drink with other people whom she found there. The soldiers told them to follow them and that they must put their feet where the feet of the soldiers are being removed, so that no one could fall in the pit or trap.

When they reached where the soldiers took them, the soldiers gave them a place to sleep. My mother was put in a room where she found a girl who had become like a mad person. My mother wanted to escape and she told the other girl who was like a mad person to go with her the girl said, there are the "Genius" who will kill us, and she said that she saw the "Genius" killing her family. My mother saw that the girl had lost her thinking senses, and she left her alone and went her way.

At last when the Genocide had ended, my mother, her sisters, and brothers lived happy life. But later one of her elder sister died after the Genocide when she had one child who was a girl. I thanked my mother for telling me a good story. This is a true story.
By

CLAIRE

3. My Hair Gives Me Knowledge

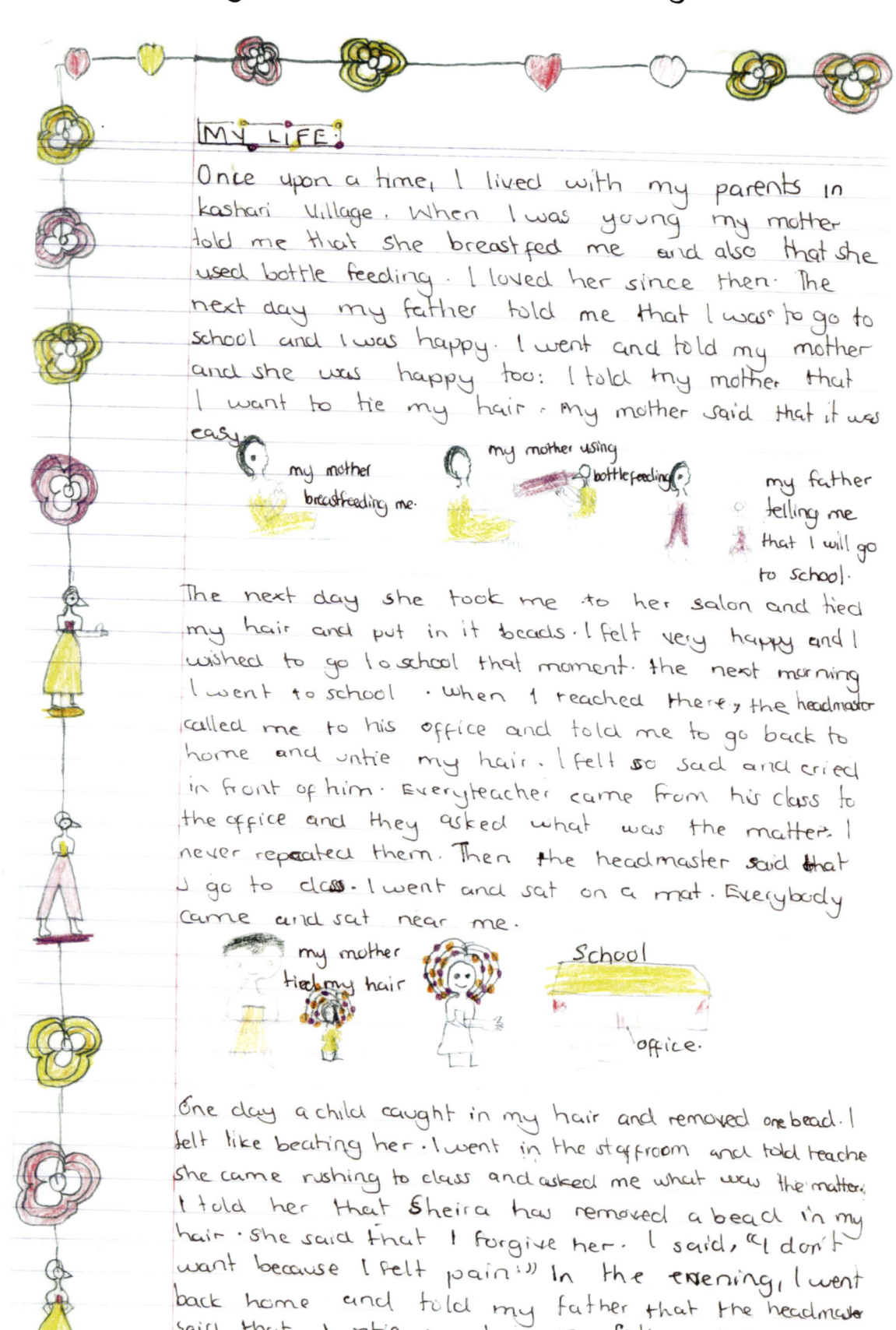

MY LIFE:

Once upon a time, I lived with my parents in Kashari village. When I was young my mother told me that she breastfed me and also that she used bottle feeding. I loved her since then. The next day my father told me that I was to go to school and I was happy. I went and told my mother and she was happy too. I told my mother that I want to tie my hair. My mother said that it was easy.

my mother breastfeeding me.

my mother using bottle feeding.

my father telling me that I will go to school.

The next day she took me to her salon and tied my hair and put in it beads. I felt very happy and I wished to go to school that moment. The next morning I went to school. When I reached there, the headmaster called me to his office and told me to go back to home and untie my hair. I felt so sad and cried in front of him. Every teacher came from his class to the office and they asked what was the matter. I never repeated them. Then the headmaster said that I go to class. I went and sat on a mat. Everybody came and sat near me.

my mother tied my hair

School office.

One day a child caught in my hair and removed one bead. I felt like beating her. I went in the staffroom and told teacher. She came rushing to class and asked me what was the matter. I told her that Sheira has removed a bead in my hair. She said that I forgive her. I said, "I don't want because I felt pain." In the evening, I went back home and told my father that the headmaster said that I untie my hair. My father asked me that who tied me the hair and I said that my mother

He told me that I go and tell my mother to untie it or to shave it. I felt so sad and I never talked to my father for a some time.

A child removing my bead

-removed bead.

staffroom

The next morning he said that I was to go back to school. I told him that I am paining the head and I also have stomachache. I quickly ran to bed.

my father telling me to go to school.

I quickly ran to bed.

He came to my bed and asked me the truth. I told him that you told me to tell my mother to shave my hair and the hair they shaved was giving me knowledge. So you want me to go to school and become the last in the whole class. Then he said that its okay that I go and tell my mum to tie me again and I said that since daddy you never studied don't also force me to study.

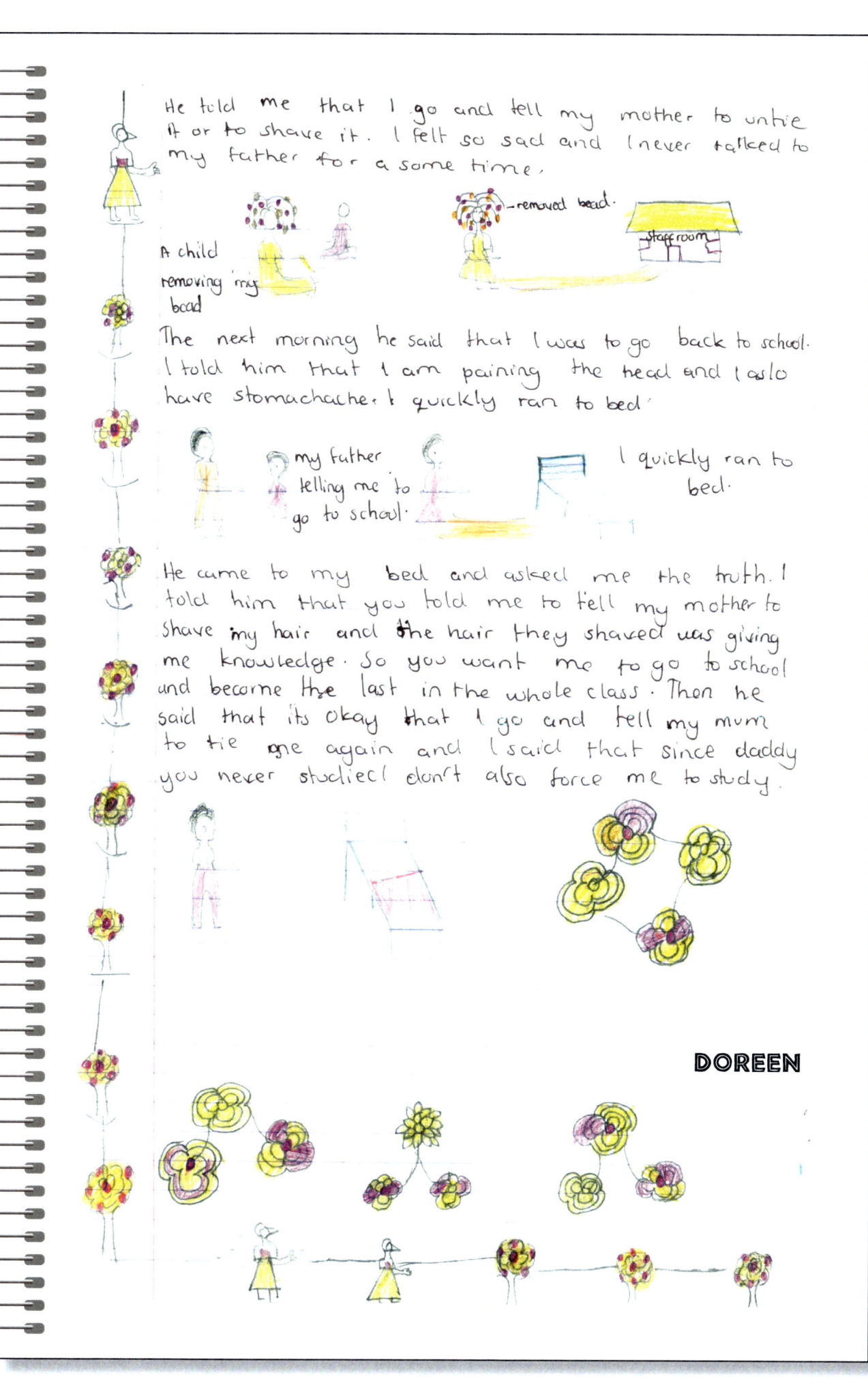

DOREEN

4. A Bag Full of Rabbit

I was born in two thousand two in Bugirii district now, I live in Jinla district.

My father died before was born, then I stayed with my mother in Bugirii. I started studying in Bugirii nursery School. After a longtime my mother took me to my aunt. It was my first time to travel. We got a bus in the morning and we reached in the evening. They were happy to see us, They prepared for us a wonderful meal. I enjoyed staying there with her and my cousins, my sister and my brother. My aunt took me to School after my mother had gone back, I was in primary one then.

I was studying with my sister and my brother in the same school. I got friends we played in the school compound I would go back home with my sister and brother when the bell rang. I wouldn't go back to School after lunch. My sister and my brother would go back to School

When I was in primary two, one day at break time I was playing with friends around primary three classroom, the bell rang.

When I was going back to class, A boy was runing to class, He knocked me down! I started crying and bleeding From the forehead.

A teacher took me and bathed me and asked me what happened. I told her and she told me to show her the boy who knocked me down. He was given a punishment and I was taken to the hospital and I had a quick recovery and I went back to School. Once my mother came to visit us. I was so happy to see her again.

PATIENCE

5. The Journey

One day, when I was four years old, My mother told to prepare myself that we are going to my grandmother's home who lived in Sembabure.

The next day, in the morning, we woke up very early. We walked until we reached the nearest trading centre. As we were standing there, a boda boda man with a motorcycle came near us and he said, madam do you need a boda boda? My mother replied yes, I need it. Since it was very near to the bus park, the boda boda man said yes and the without counting the child, I will take you for one thousand shillings only. My mother replied 'yes', you can take us. When we reached the bus park, most of the buses were still there

A black skinned man came closer to us before we got off the motorcycle. The black skinned man asked us where we were going. My mother replied, we are going to Sembabure near the mosque. The black skinned man who was the bus driver said that without counting the luggage you will pay me ten thousand shillings only. My mother said that she had eight thousand shillings. The bus driver replied, It is okay.

We entered the bus there were very many but still the driver wanted other passengers. We started travelling. When we were travelling, a woman besideds, said that most drivers want money thats why they make us too congested. We travelled and travelled. When we reached in a certain centre, she moved outside and brought bread and two bottles of pineapple juice and then we continued travelling. When we reached the mosque, the bus stopped and we got out. My mother paid the conductor and we went to my grandmother's home. When we reached there, they were ready for us and they welcomed us nicely. My grandfather had kept yellow bananas. He brought them and and gave them to us. My grandmother had already prepared food. We ate and drunk. After we had finished eating, They started telling us stories.

EILEEN

6. Violence Remembered

MY LIFE:

I was born in Isingiro. My mother told me about the war of Uganda fighting for being a president. Amin was the President who behaved poorly he never liked his people. Wherever he met a girl he would rape her. When the war started he would get a sharp stick he makes the father to sleep down and the mother plus children to pierce them until they died then he would call the soliders to carry them into them into vehicle.

That time Amin would eat people as wild animals. Most people escaped to other countries to protect their lifes.
After the war people came back in there districts. People started digging and planting crops so as to get food for eating but people who were escaping destoryed there crops.

After sometime the war had stopped, Amin said that let me go to visit my people. As he reached their he was welcomed. At the end of the meeting he thanked them. He entered the aroplane, and said to the people of Kabale. People of Kabale you are vegetable growers. People became so surprised !!!!!!!!!!!!

Our President is abusing us. He even visited England and said to the Queen of England that let me adress you by removing the testors and then say my speech
THAT IS THE END OF MY STORY: LYNN

7. The Boy Who Knocked Me Down

MY LIFE

I was born in two thousand two in Buginii district now, I live in Jinja district.

My father died before I was born, then I stayed with my mother in Buginii. I started studying in Buginii nusery school. After a longtime my mother took me to my aunt. It was my first time to travel. We got a bus in the morning and we reached in the evening. They were happy to see us. They prepared for us a wonderful meal. I enjoyed staying there with her and my cousins, my sister and my brother. My aunt took me to school after my mother had gone back, I was in primary one then.

I was studying with my sister and my brother in the same school. I got friends we played in the school compound. I would go back home with my sister and my brother when the bell rang. I wouldn't go back to school after lnch. My sister and my brother would go back to school.

When I was in primary two, One day at break time I was playing with my friends around primary three classroom, the bell rang. When I was going back to class, A boy was runing to class, He knocked me down! I started crying and bleeding from the forehead.

A teacher took me and bathed me and asked me what happened. I told her and she told me to show her the boy who knocked me down. He was given a punishment and I was taken to the hospital and I had a quick recovery and I went back to school. Once my mother came to visit us. I was so happy to she her again.

ESME

8. Hunger

MY LIFE

Four years ago, there was hunger in our village. What my mother used to do, she would cook for us millet and beans untill another type of food came in our village.

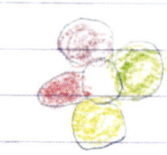

My mother mingling millet.

Some people used to drink tea and they sleep. But others had nothing. They would sleep on empty stomachs. By that time, there was a man called kasiwi and her wife kyomugisha. They didn't have enough food. They would go to every family looking for food.

What people would tell them was that, how she is that's how others are. Some of us would not eat millet but we would eat it because of hunger. Because it was a season of famine, many people had no food.

But two years later things changed. People got food but others had no food. So others who had no food would go to ask the ones who had food.

But now in some parts of our village, still people don't have food but at least they are feeling well but not like the

When I was in school, I studed when I was three years old. Children used to tease me but I would not say anything. The headteacher told the teacher that I had not finished the school fees. I was chased. By that time, I was in primary two. My father told me to sit that I will go with the school fees the next day to school.

When I was crying because they sent me home for school fees.

I was unhappy but I kept quiet. The next day I went to school and I studed my primary two class. The next year, I was promoted to primary three when I came to coloma primary school.

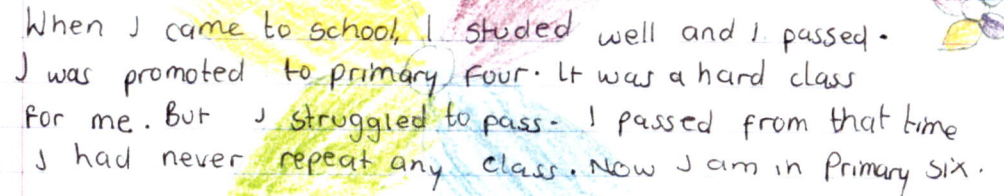

When I came to school, I studed well and I passed. I was promoted to primary four. It was a hard class for me. But I struggled to pass. I passed from that time I had never repeat any class. Now I am in Primary six.

People in our village are very happy that they nolonger eat millet and beans these days. From that time, people are happy that hunger is nolonger there.

By: HELEN

9. Reward For a Monkey Restored

> MY LIFE

When I was a little girl of seven years, I lived with my parents. I was excited to go to school. When I joined Primary five, I started revising hard. I got a prize for being the second in class and I was so excited I could not believe it! When I reached home, my parents were happy and they asked me where I would like to have my holidays. I said that I wanted to visit my uncle who lives near Queen Elizabeth National Park. Oh! it was alot of fun there. He lived in a flat where I could see everything. I saw a lion, Monkey, Elephant and a zebra. At night we enjoyed meat of a Uganda cob, matooke and rice.

I was receiving a prize from the headteacher

In the morning, we found a monkey in the house. It had escaped from the National park. It was the first time to touch a baby monkey. It was quite interesting and funny. I asked if I could take it back to the National Park. He said yes, and I ran carrying it. On the way, I found two squirrels crossing the road. I stood and took a look at them. I proceeded with the journey. I reached the reception and told them that I had a monkey which had escaped. They were happy that the monkey was back. They asked me what I wanted. I told them that I wanted to tour the National park. They hired a jeep and took me as they explained while asking questions. I was suprised a game ranger threw five yellow bananas to a monkey. It grabed them and ate them in a hurry. I saw monkeys, Tigers, Lions, Leopards, Kingfishers and bush buck. We finished the tour and we drove back to the reception. I bought an ice cream and went back home happily.

A game ranger throwing yellow bananas.

My uncle asked, " Where have you been?" I narrated the whole story. He said "Your are kind my child." So I asked my uncle to take me to the beach. He accepted and took me to the beach which was near a zoo I saw a snake when we reached the beach, I found there my two best friends Elishu and Mercy. My uncle gave me money and I went with my friends to the canteen. I bought nodles, icecream, cake and one bottle of juice. I enjoyed swimming and I had alot of fun with my uncle and friends. In the evening, I had to go back home. I found when they had prepared a glass of juice and cookies I was thirsty I drank two glasses and ate four cookies.

Me and my uncle at the beach.

The next day as we were going back home in Mbarara, I saw people selling potatoes, mangoes and yellow bananas. My uncle bought for me mangoes which were delicious. Even they bought for our family yellow bananas and potatoes. When we reached Mbarara town, he bought for me, my sister and my two brothers clothes and shoes. He bought two sacks of rice, bread, wheat flour, a box of glasses, a suit for my father and a dress for my mother. When I arrived at home my parents were happy to see me and they gave me food to eat and I drank juice. My uncle spent one night at home and in the morning, he went back to his home in Kasese. It was a nice holiday for me.

My parents happy to see me.

HOPE

10. The Day My Father Died

MY LIFE:

Once upon a time. I was four years old. I went to school for my first time. When I reached there, I was confused. I never knew where to releive myself from. I started crying. The teacher asked me, What was the matter? I told her that I wanted to releive myself. She took me. From then, I learnt where to releive myself from when I am at school. When it came to the middle of the term, the headmaster came in classes chasing pupils who never paid school fees. He sent me home to bring school fees. When I reached there, I found my father and my mother were not there. I sat near the door and started crying. When I was there, our neighbour found me there crying and told me that my parents have gone to the hospital. Our neighbour gave me food to eat and I ate it. I told her about the school fees. She gave ten thousand shillings and I took it at school. When I reached at school, I asked my fellow pupils where the headmaster's office was. I went there and gave him the school fees and I went back to class

When it came to the time of going home, I went home and found there many people sitting. I never asked what had happened? I went to play with my cousin sisters and brothers. We could pour sand on our heads and on the face. When five minutes had past by, I saw people crying and my aunt was also crying. She was carrying my sister who was also crying. When I asked her what had happened, she told me that my father had died. I never went back to comfort my mother. I just went back to play.

CONTENT

11. My Trip to the Lake

Once upon a time when I was eight years old, I asked my father to visit Lake Mburo National Park, he told me to organise a special Saturday to go there. When the Saturday came, we had some visitors at home, so we could not go.

My father had already prepared the money and a car to take us. He said sorry to me. I slept crying that night. In the morning, my mother made me to bathe, take breakfast and go to church. The following Saturday morning my father and I bathed, took breakfast, and set off for the journey. It was my first time to travel in a car. I saw plants moving and felt like vomiting. My father asked me what was wrong. I said that I saw plants moving and felt sick. He stopped and bought for me a cake, a bottle of soda and a story book to help me to stop looking outside as the car moved.

We then arrived at Lake Nabarro at 1:00pm in the afternoon, I saw different animals I was excited; my father took some pictures of them.

I saw a lion and cried very loudly, the game ranger scared it away. As we went on moving, I saw a baboon eating a banana like a person, and I laughed. When I got tired I asked my father to take me home. When we entered, I looked at the animal pictures, it was a very wonderful day in my life.

CELIA

12. My Hair

At one time, I lived with my father, mother, brothers and my grandparents. I told my mother that I wanted to go to school, with my hair plaited. She immediately took me to the salon and plaited my hair, the next day I went to school. When I reached the school, I was the only pupil with plaited hair. Many pupils looked at me, and some even followed me.

When it was time for pupils to go home, the headmaster called me and told me not to go back to school with plaited hair. I was very sad and cried in front of him. I asked him why but he just walked away.

On that day, I did not tell my mother what the headmaster had told me because, I loved my plaited hair. I went back to school in the morning and the headmaster chased me back home. When I reached home, I told my mother that the headmaster did not want me with plaited hair at school. Mother immediately took me to the salon and unplaited my hair.

I was very sad.

I went back to school crying that morning, because my hair was unplaited. I went to the classroom sad. The timekeeper rang the bell after some minutes and pupils went back home. I told my mother that I did not want to go back to that school. I did not go back the next day. After some weeks, I was brought to Coloma Primary School. I am very happy now.

MONA

PART TWO:
A Tale I Was Told

13. Everybody Has The Right to a Name

MY LIFE

Once upon a time, I was living at home with my grandmother. One afternoon as we had finished taking lunch, I asked her to tell me a story. And she told me a story which goes like this:

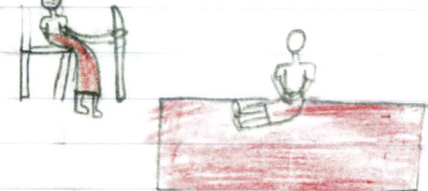

Long ago there lived a man and his wife. They had three children namely Birungi, Mugisha and the last born was not yet baptised. But because she grew to the age of two years without a name, people wanted to know her name. Her parents decided to call her Kebirungi as her family name.

When Kebirungi grew up, she was not happy with her name. She never asked why they called her that name because she thought it was her real name. Kebirungi always complained about how bad and boring her name was. Whenever anybody called her, she asked why they decided to call her that name. One day her brother Mugisha called and Kebirungi asked him, "Why do you call me that name again and again?" Her brother was tired of her sister complaining about her boring name and then he decided to tell her the truth. When Kebirungi was told the truth, she decided to ask her parents. Eventhough her brother and sister told her not to do so, Kebirungi still insisted to ask.

One day as they were taking lunch, her mother asked her to go and get some juice for the family. But Kebirungi refused saying, before you tell me the truth, I will not go. Her sister and brother were suprised to hear that because they thought she was just joking.

"Which truth?" Asked her mother. "Was I baptised?" Asked Kebirungi. Kebirungi's parents were ashamed and not happy because they immediately thought that her brother and sister had told her the truth. "I don't want to be called Kebirungi again. If I were you, I would stop asking because that is your name and it will remain yours." Said her sister.
Her sister said so in order to convice her parents. You are saying that because you have a name and you are not nameless like me. Said Kebirungi. "What do you say father?" Shall I remain nameless? asked Kebirungi. Do not mind, you will be baptised soon but we need to first give you a family name, said her father. I don't want any name apart from my christian name, said Kebirungi. Then her parents had to prepare for her baptism day soon. Kebirungi did not even do a single work at home. When her mother asked why she didn't want to do anything she always said that nameless children are the ones who are young and young children do not do work.

PETAL

14. Is God in America?

Once upon a time, there was a man called John. He had no wife but one day he got a wife. The wife bore a child who was dumb and deaf. One day, when a robber attacked them. He came at their home as if he was touring, but he was seeing where he will pass when stealing.

Afterwards he went back to his home gently. When he reached at his home, he told other people who were killers to kill the man and the wife. As the man was repairing the car, the robbers came gently and slowly and shot him. While the mother was coming to get the child to eat, the mother saw the robbers. She ran very fast and hid herself and the child in a house. Then she got a panga knife.

When the robbers entered in the house, they searched for the wife and the child and after the robbers found the wife, and killed her while the child was watching them. The robbers stole the money and went away. After wards the child went out of the house and went on the street. A drunkard man came across the street and saw a young child having like four years, so he decided to take the child. He took the child and taught him some signs like dumb people always do.

But the robbers recalled that there was a child who was watching them when killing the parents. They searched for the child but the child had a strong man who would guard the child, but the robbers had tricks. The robbers sent a man to lie to the strong man, that the child was calling him sweet daddy, but a strong man pushed him out. The robbers also sent another man, but the strong man also defeated him.

At last, the police caught the robbers and they were sentenced to death. But the child was unhappy because he had no parents. So I thank God for having my parents alive. Even though people say that he is in America, I can also go there to praise him and to thank him.

ALWAYS THANK GOD FOR WHAT YOU HAVE

CHARITY

15. The Big Animal Who Taught Manners

When I was very young, my mother told me that when she was a young child there was war in their village. And when she saw that it had reached in their village she hid in a hole, and they never saw her, so she survived. When the war was over my grandfather died because of cancer.

When I was very young my grandmother told me that there lived a very big animal which could teach children good manners. Now once my grandmother took my mother to that animal, because she liked crying. When they took her it beat her, and she started learning good manners.

When I was young my mother told me another story about a snake. Once upon a time there lived a very big snake and that snake could eat children who were greedy, badly behaved and not obeying their parents. Now once there were four girls whom they had sent to the well to bring some water. When they were going the snake saw them and called them and said, "come to my house". Then the snake took them to its house and gave them pieces of meat. One of these girls was greedy so she ate the meat. Then later the snake said, "all of you give me my pieces of meat", the three girls gave them back to the snake and the other ones never had any meat. After others ran outside and the other one stayed in the snake's house. And now after some years the snake married the girl, and they produced children.

When I was still very young my mother told me that I liked drinking milk, so every day I could tell my mother that I want milk and she could give it to me. And my other sisters, one of them liked passion fruits and another one liked soda. So that's the end of my story.

KITTY

16. Itching

My Life

Long time ago I was borne in kashari but I grew up from my grandmother's home and she loved me so much because I was a handworking girl I usually wake up early in the morning I sweep the house, compound and cook milk.

When I was six years old my grandmother told me astroy about the party that she attended she started telling me that there were three boys their names are James, Andrew and kitineli, they usually drink alcholo and the oner of the party refused to give them alcholo. The boys became sad and went in the farm and collected the enyyenyi and put them in the leaves that were in the latrine. It was at 7:00 p.m when the men had finished to eat.

One man went to visit a latrine after visiting a latrine he got some leaves in the latrine and cleaned himself when he was tieing his belt, he had something itiching him and the man started saying oh-- my God what has happen. The man run to the farm and started scratching himself on the hill.

The another man went to visit a latrine after when he had finished to visit a latrine he got some leaves to clean himself the engyenyi started itiching him the man said what has happen oh-- my The man ran to the farm and started scratching on the hill when he was on the hill he saw his friend there also scratching himself on the hill, he asked his friend what has happen John told him that he doesn't know.

The oner of the party would see when the people who could go in the latrien when they are not coming back. What has happen to my people. He went to see whas has happen. He found when the men are very busy scratching themselves the man told them that they were the three boys who did this because of alcholo.

PRUDENCE

17. The Green Snake

MY LIFE
THE TITLE OF MY STORY IS ABOUT MY GRANDMOTHER.
I was born from kashari. And my grandmother was born from Rwapala.

Once upon a time there lived a grandmother in the village called kashari. Her house was built with grass one day, I went to visit her. I found her cooking meat. She asked me what I can eat? I told her that I can eat pork. The grandmother started saying why I can't eat meat? I answered that when I was growing up I was not eating meat. When she knew that I was not eating meat she went to the market and brought pork. When she reached home, she entered the house while she was entering in the house, she saw a snake. And the snake was big in size and tall. The grandmother was so sad to see the snake and for me I was crying because I had never saw a snake and when I went back home, My mother asked me what has happened and I told her that I had seen a snake which I had never seen.

When my mother was asking the colour of the snake, she saw a snake which was green in colour. It was moving from the bush entering in the house. My mother looked for the stick to kill it when she went in the house to kill the snake it turned into a person. I went running to call people. When people reached there, the snake turned into a person and started talking then after it had finished to talk it again turned into a snake. When my father came asked what has happened? My mother had no words to say. Then my father entered in the house he found a person sitting on the chair when he was going to greet he found when it was a snake.
This is the end of my story
BY
MARY

18. A Christmas Tale

Once upon a time, during my life holidays in the third term last year when I was from school, my father came and picked me from school in his car. I was the last child to come at home. The day I reached home we drank tea with bread, at night we ate pork with matooke we watched television, after we slept. Like after two weeks we were preparing to go to the village with my father, mother, sisters and brothers, but my aunt never came with us because she wanted to go for Christmas with her parents.

On Christmas day in the morning, we waked up and washed our faces and brushed teeth. After we drunk tea with bananas, maize, groundnuts, bread with blueband and zesta. After we dressed for Church to pray. In the Church, we were many people with new dresses, skirts, shirts and shoes. I was very happy to see all my village friends and new friends who were my cousins and aunts. After Christmas service, all children were given balloons. At lunch, we ate meat of a sheep, chicken, matooke, chips and sodas. One time, I asked my grandfather to tell me a story about our farm. He said "One day, there were big trees which people said that monkeys lived there". But when I heard of this, I never believed it. He continued and said that, "One morning there was a man fetching water, the man was called Mukasa Peter. That man saw an animal from a tree, he tried to extend behind and even the monkey which wanted to beat a man. The man ran quickly and left the monkey which was near a river. That was the end of the story. The next day we went at home in Mbarara, like after four weeks. I went to school to study, so this holiday was good to me, and I am at school ready to study for my education.

SACHA

19. Boo Learns a Lesson

When I was a little girl, I was short and funny. I used to make fun of other children. One day, I learnt how to behave well. I learnt it from my teacher. My teacher told us a story about "Boo the lazy one".

Boo was a very lazy boy. He liked to play one day, Boo's grandmother became ill. His mother was walking from the market she had bought for Boo a ball. He was very happy.

He went outside to play and he was shouting Mother said "Will you stop shouting, Boo. Boo said "yes mummy", but he didn't stop shouting. Mother said Boo, "go and bring medicine for your grand mother". Boo went and the rain started. Boo was about to reach the doctors place, but he went home to get an umbrella. He went back to get the medicine. On his way back home, he fell in the water. He walked slowly. When he reached home he found when they had already gone to the hospital. Boo started crying. From then Boo learnt a lesson. Not be disobedient and slow.

DENISE

20. Pots

Once upon a time, there lived a girl in a small village of Mukono. The girl's name was called Taaka. Her father was called Mulongi. Mulongi had eight children and he was the best potter in the whole village. People liked his pots. They were beautiful. One day Mulongi made for his children, pots. He told them to go and fetch water at the well. He told them many times that any one broke her pot. "He will take her to Cheeche. Cheeche will eat her– Cheeche will kill her". One day, when Taaka was going with her sisters to the well she broke her pot and started crying. She never went back home, she went to Cheeche's home. On her way she met a man and his wife digging in their garden. They were very tired, they asked her for help. She caught the hoe and started digging up to the end. Then they thanked her. When she was going to continue with her journey, the man told her a secret. "When you are going, you will get me yellow bananas and meat on the way, don't eat any thing of those". Then she continued. She met yellow bananas, they said "Come and eat us". Then she said "I cannot do so I am going at Cheeche's home". After a hour she met meat in the saucepan and it said "Come and eat us". She said "I cannot do so, I am going to Cheeche's home". Then she reached Cheeche's home. She found the other beasts were pouring rubbish. They told her to move and she said that she was not clean enough, they could do so. They wanted to test her behaviour.

FERN

21. The Sack

MY LIFE.

I was born in Rwanda in a district called Kabuye. I am the third girl in our family. My mother told me that when I was still young I could sleep for a long time. When I was about three years, I went with my elder sister and my cousin sister to collect firewood. On our way, we saw a cross. We were scared and we ran away. When we told our parents, they could not what we were saying. After some time, we migrated. When we were in our new house, I once entered my parent's room and saw a snake. I never knew it's real name and so I said I have seen an earthworm. I jumped away from the bed and told my father. He came with a big stick and killed it. When I was once in the chair, I saw like a star calling me, when I saw it then calling me, I started to go pushing my head and arms, so that I can get it, when I went to get it, I beat my head on the arm chair and I cried.

When I was in my holiday, my mother told me a story of a hare. That long ago there lived a hare it would hunt animals and eat them but when his friends tried to ask where he moved his food, he could fool them. One day Mr. Elephant went to ask Mr. Hare where moved his food and he said that he always cut the meat from his batock. When the elephant heard that, it also went and did the same thing. Another day, tiger came to Mr. Hare to ask him him the same questions, he fooled him, he told it that if you hear a stone with a small sound you move away and if you a stone with a loud sound you lay infront of it and the stone fell on it's back. It made itself as if it was dead.

When hare came to see whether tiger was dead, Mr. Hare found him laying down and it bought a sack for putting in the tiger in his sack, he went home, On his way home he met the tortoise. Mr. Hare asked the tortoise to help him carry the sack, Mr. tortoise accepted, when he was carrying a sack, he had something pinching him, he said are these red ants or. He did not bother about that, when he reached in Mr. Hare's house, he kept there the sack. When it was in the evening, Mr. Hare came to his home. People who live here how are you? But nothing answered him. He was trying to know if there would be something in his house. He again said, "people who live here how are you? Then the tiger answered we are fine. Then Mr. Hare said "I know that you also want to eat me, I have know you, you are Mr. Tiger, then Mr. Hare ran away.

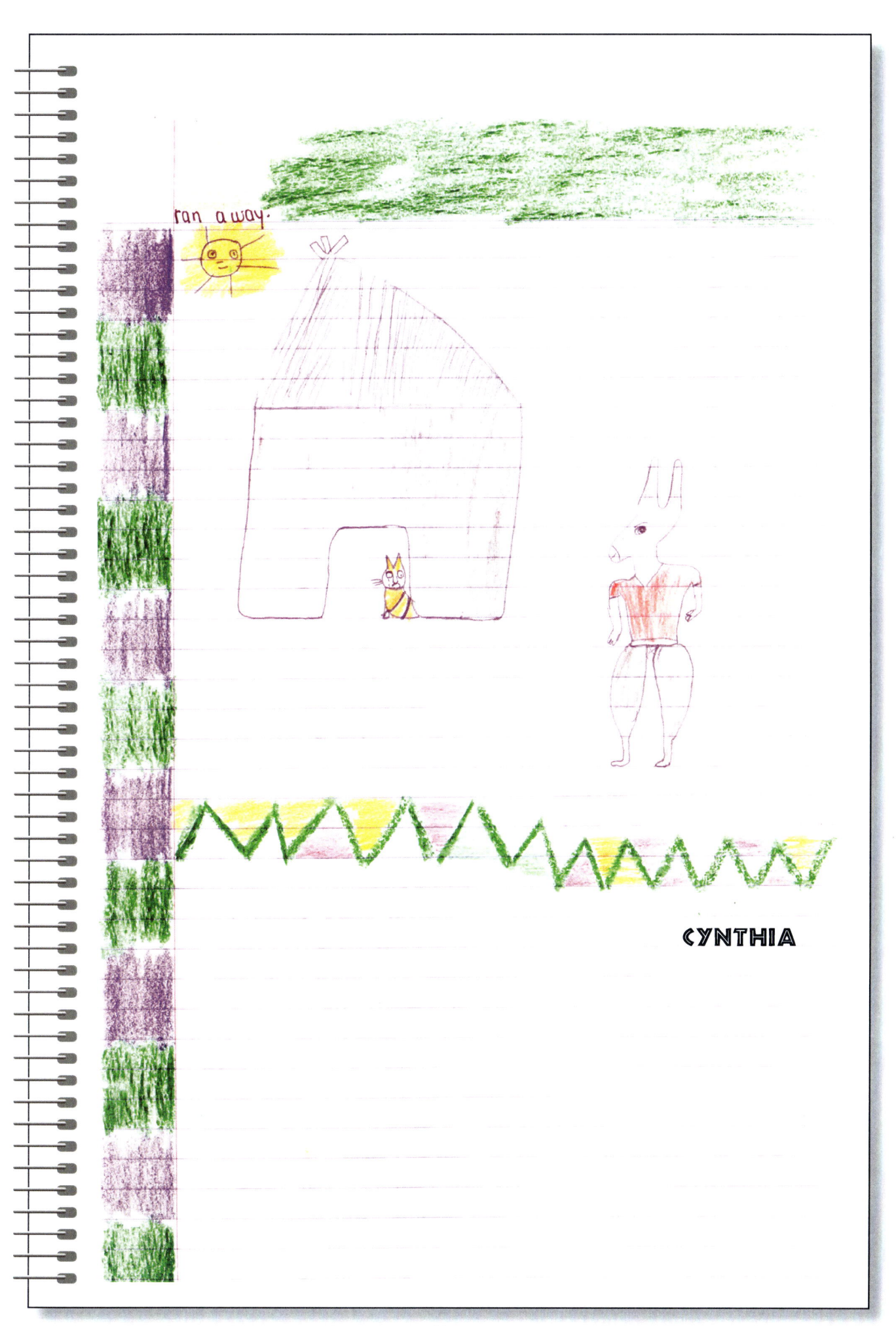

CYNTHIA

22. The Story of Luke

Once upon a time, there was a boy called Lule he was ten years old. Lule went to fetch water and Seera swept the house. The mother of Lule and Seera went to their mother to show them their piece of land. Their mother was to plant some seeds according to the following: peas, beans and groundnuts. Seera chose to plant peas on her smallest piece of land. Lule chose the largest piece of land to plant beans.

One Monday Lule told his mother that he wants to go to the hospital because he was suffering from malaria, Seera asked, "Lule are you seriously sick? What did your mother give you?" Lule said, "Mother, she has given me the herbal medicine". Peter and Paul came to visit Lule's home. Peter bought for Lule Five thousand shillings, Peter bought for Lule some basic needs. Lule got healed on Friday. Peter and paul came to collect Lule to go and play Football.

Lule was a goalkeeper, Seera and Peter lived together whilst Sarah was about to score. Peter kicked the ball to score but Paul got it. Lule came seriously and kicked the ball he scored Paul.

PATRICA

23. Bad Behaviour

Once upon a time, there was a girl called Kaitesi. She was very beautiful, but very badly behaved. Kaitesi had her sister called Bonny. Bonny was well behaved. Kaitesi's parents loved her, but she did not love them as much. She used to abuse her parents. One day, she went to visit her aunt Patricia.

Aunt Patricia loved her, but she did not know that she was badly behaved. One day Kaitesi destroyed many things like glasses and plates. She even refused to study. The next morning, she went back to her home.

When some days passed, she went to the bush to collect firewood.

She found a baboon, she disturbed it and it ran away. When she met a mother monkey on the way. The mother monkey was eating mangoes and she wanted to steal some, but the monkey caught her.

When the monkey caught her, it tied her on the rope and started beating her. When it stopped beating her, she escaped and ran crying. Since that time she has started behaving very well, and respects her parents.

NITA

24. Snake Bite

One day, I went in the banana plantation to cut the banana fruit. As I was cutting a banana fruit, the big black snake came on a banana plant. It entered my skirt ,and it bite me on the thigh. I cried but nobody heard me. There was an old woman passing, when she heard me crying, she come near me to help me, but the snake had run. The old women took me home. I had tied grass on my thigh. My mother took me to the hospital and doctors treated me. And I got healed that night. My mother told me that I pack my clothes, that I was going to visit my aunt. We woke up early and prepared ourselves, and we boarded a bus at a bus park. We started the journey .I saw interesting things on the way. When we reached my aunts place she welcomed us and told us to sit in the sitting room. We drank milk and we ate bread. After eating and drinking we went to bath, after bathing we watched cartoons, and after we went to sleep. The next morning we went in the market and we brought clothes, and we went back home. On Monday my parents had gone to the garden. And my mother had left me home to cook matooke only, and my mother was to cook meat. When my mother returned from the garden, she went in the kitchen to see how I had cooked. She found the meat wasn't there. She asked me where it had gone. I told her that I don't know. She beat me I cried, and then I went to my grandmothers place. And my grandmother asked me what had happened. I told her that my mother had beaten me, and later she asked me why had she beaten me. I said nothing. And my grandmother came at home but my grandmother never knew how to speak. She would talk words, which you wouldn't hear. When my grandmother went home my mother started abusing me. When my father returned from town, I told him that my mother had beaten me and my father told me that he will beat her. I said that I forgive her, and my sisters laughed at me. After when we had our supper and we slept. In the morning I greeted her and she told me that I am fine my daughter. Then she took me in the shop and she gave me a cake and a soda Fanta.

MARIA

25. Uganda at War

MY LIFE

Once upon a time in my life, I heard a story about the early years, like the years which my father was born that there was a war in our country uganda.

One day their came soldiers in our country uganda. Those soldiers were in the time when President Iddi Amin Dada was in power. He ruled People of uganda harshly. While ruling the people of Uganda harshly, he also sent soldiers and his wife in the aeroplane to start the war; the aeroplane would cut all the top parts of the trees and People of Uganda would fear and start hiding.

While starting the war, the woman just feared and went back to her husband President Idd Amin Dada, when the woman reached there, she told him what had happened. When she told him, he was not happy. He asked, "how can you fear such a small and short war. He got angry and shot the woman to death.

The Soliders went to a place called kagarama in Ntugamo district where my mother was born and raped women and young girls.
One day the soldiers came to a home of a certain man and asked him, "do you have a wife?", "No I don't have a wife".

He answered deceiving them. He had a wife and the wife had a baby. As the man was deceiving, the baby cried in the house under the bed. The soldiers lit the torch under the bed and pulled the woman out and raped her as the man was watching and crying. After raping the woman the man said that, "I can not again marry that woman to spread to me the diseases of the soldiers".

When the Soldiers moved away from kagarama after disturbing the people of kagarama, my grandfather had taken the five children of his to another district which had Peace for them not to be raped because the soldiers who ask people of kagarama that, "Who has intelligent and beautiful girls is this county", people would say my grandfather has very intelligent and beautiful girls in this county.

He had taken them with another man with his wife and his eight children. When the war was finished they bought them back and they left chicken food like Posho and some mash to eat

the time they came back they found when they had multiplied hens. When they came back they were eating like people who had never seen food because the Place where they had been had little food. The time they got enough food they lived a happy and good way.

KUNA

26. The Witch Doctor

MY LIFE

My mother always tell me that when I was just young. I used to stay with my grandma. The day my mother brought me, I started my studies. When I was in Primary four, I went back to my grandma's home. The night I was she told me that there was war between the Banyankole and the Baganda. My grandma lost a son in the war but she was a humble woman. When the war ended they had displaced their houses. They never had food for the family because the father could not be at home but the mother tried to care for her children.

Telling stories
fire

Once upon a time theire lived a rich man in their village he used to have demonies. He used to work as a witch doctor. He would poison people in the village.

Uganda Flag

On day the man died and then he was burnt by the natives of the village. He never wanted others to have things all the peoples where happy for his death

One woman poisoned my cousin brother with charcoal of the dead witch doctor. and he died. I am ending my story saying that we should love others as we love our selves.

PEACE

27. Mr. Hare

Once in my life style, my grandmother and grand father used to tell me stories about some animals and birds. They told me how animals became friends to each other and how some animals became enemies after some years.

When I would come from school, I would just go to grandfathers home and I would not do any kind of work at home. I would just come to sleep because my grandmother could give me food. When I would reach home, my mother would punish me and the next day, she would refuse that I may not go there.

One day, my grand mother told me a story about hare and the woman. She told me that once upon a time, there lived Mr. Hare, who was a lazy animal without a garden, where she would get food from. One dry season, Mr. Hare was very hungry looking for food. He went in the forest looking for food but he could not find it. He found only animals but he couldn't eat meat.

Mr. Hare kept on going looking for food in the gardens. Mr. Hare met Mr. Mokey and asked him to help him but Mr. Monkey had no food. Mr Hare kept on looking food and met a woman who had a basket & millet seeds

The woman gave Mr. Hare the millet seeds to go and plant them. Mr. Monkey just went and ate the seeds but he never planted them.

After two weeks, Mr. Hare met the woman, the woman asked Hare if the millet is growing very well. Mr. Hare told the woman that he spends the whole day watering and weeding the millet. The woman thanked Hare for the great work he was doing. After two month, the woman went to Hare's house and ask Hare to show her the garden of millet. Mr. Hare took the woman to the neighbours garden of millet. The woman started cutting the millet and Mr. Hare ran away. The owner of the garden came running and caught the woman. The man started beating the women. After two days, the woman started looking for Mr. Hare.

BANI

28. The Right Decision

Once upon a time in our villiage, there lived a man who worked hard and he was called Peter. He married a woman called Jane after some time Jane produced twins a boy and a girl. They named the girl Joan and the boy John. The twins liked each other and also liked their parents equally. They performed well and also worked hard.

Suddenly, their mother died when they were in Primary six. They buried her and continued studying. Years passed and they were in senior six. The boy and the girl were well behaved but because of the boy's bad friends he chose a bad decision. The bad decision was that he joined a gang. When her sister knew that he had joined that gang, she tried to warn him but the boy never listened. After lunch when John was with his friends he told them what Joan had told him. They laughed and laughed. One of his friends called James told him that she (Joan) wanted you to be lonely. They finished senior six with good marks but when John and Joan went back home John stole big things like money, sheep, goats etc.

Unfortunately their father died of malaria but that did not change John's behaviour. On Friday morning he woke up very early and went to steal from the richest person in the whole village, who was called Joseph. But when he went to steal the guards of Joseph's house caught him.

The guards of Joseph's house took him to the prison. After a few months he was taken to court and was sentenced to death and they burnt him. So always choose the right decision.

REGINA

29. The Broken Cup

MY LIFE.

When I was 5 years old, my mother told me never to touch her cup, because I would break it and I obeyed.

One day, my sister told me to take it for her and I refused. She forced me because she was older than me.

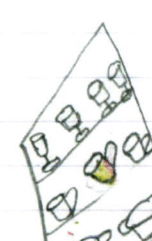

She wanted my mother to beat me because my mother had never beaten me.
I just took it for her and it did not break.
The second time when my sister had not told me anything, I also got the cup and put it down.
I thought that my mother was deceiving me that her cup would break.
The next time, I threw the cup up and failed to hold it.

When it fell down and broke, I started shivering.
I went and hid under the bed.

My mother called me when she heard that something had fallen down.
When I refused to reply, my mother came.
She found that her cup had broken.
She was angry and wanted to beat me up.
She called me and I went.
As soon as she brought the stick, I started saying what had happened.

She forgave me and called my sister.
My mother asked her why she wanted me to take for her the cup, she kept quiet.
My mother started beating her. I learn not to disobey my parents and not to follow what other people tell me to do that is bad.

⭐ TELLING THE TRUTH IS GOOD ☆

TINA

30. The Slave

One day a man and his wife had one child her name was Kisaake. As she got older, her father died in an accident. Then Kisaake has lived with her mother.

One afternoon an huge beast came long asking for shelter because there was no food for it.

One morning the mother of Kisaake was going to the market. Kisaake's mother told the beast to never eat her daughter.

The beast replied "I won't." As Kisaake woke up, immediately the beast ran away. As the mother of Kisaake came back, she asked where it had gone. Kisaake had nothing in answer.

SOPHIE

31. The Elephant and the Gorilla

Once upon a time, the elephant and the gorilla were best friends. They lived in a thick bush where there were no other animals except the two friends. After a month, the two friends gave birth to young ones, the elephant had one baby, the gorilla had seven.

Early in the morning as the sun was rising, the gorilla told the elephant to go and look for food for the two of them and their young ones. So the elephant went and went. She saw the maize garden. She was overjoyed to see maize growing very well without anyone destroying it. She harvested seven maize for gorilla's young ones and one for her young one, one for the gorilla and lastly one for herself.

She then ran as first as she could. When she reached home, she found the fellows sleeping. She was shocked about what had happened during the day playing with the young ones for five hours.

The elephant then deceived the gorilla that she had bought delicious grapes. So the gorilla woke up and asked the elephant why she would deceive her. The elephant and the gorilla and the whole family sat down and ate. They then lived peacefully.

DESIRE

32. Kanyeyite The Old Man

I was born in Rukiri sub-county in Ibanda district. When I grew up, I found out that my grandfather was already dead but the other grandparents of mine were still alive.

Whenever we finished having supper, we would all gather in one place and tell stories to each other. One day, my grandfather told us a nice and interesting story. We were all happy.

The story was: 'Kanyeyite the Old Man'.

There was once an old man called Kanyeyite. He had no food to eat. One day, as he was walking around Mr. Kikoko's home, he saw a knife and ran to Kikoko and told him that he was going to kill himself. Mr. Kikoko supported Mr. Kanyeyite because he knew he was going to get food for his supper. Mr. Kanyeyite ended up killing himself.

When I grew up, my mother told me that I was going to go to school. I was happy because I would always tell her that I also wanted to go to school. Every morning I would wake up lay my bed, wash my face, take my breakfast and go to school because I was a day student. When I completed primary one, I was taken to another school where I joined primary two in 2010. I am now in primary six at the same school. I am proud of my school.

ANNA

33. Jane and Joan

MY LIFE STORY.

The story I am going to write was told to me by my grandfather when I was six years old. I asked him to tell me a story and he narrated to me.

Once upon a time there lived a man and his wife. The man was called Kasano and the wife was called Sandrah. They had two daughters.

Their daughters were called Jane and Joan. Jane was in senior six while Joan was in senior five. They loved their father most because he used to pay school fees for them.

After they had finished university, they went back home and their father welcomed them happily.

Jane and Joan being welcomed by their father.

After two weeks, their father suffered from malaria. Quickly he was rushed to the hospital. After six months, their father died.

After the burrial, they started searching for jobs.

Two months later, they got jobs and started struggling to work hard. Everybody liked them because of being hardworking people. Six months later, they started a primary school which was so nice and good that everybody liked it.

End by VIC

34. Legs

MY LIFE

THE STORY ABOUT THE MAN WHO HAD WOUNDS ON THE LEG.

One upon a time there lived a man with two wives. The man had wounds on his legs. One day, He sent one of his child to look for him the medicine from an old woman who lived far way in the bush. The child went and stayed on the road for two days.

The boy going to look for the medicine for his father.

On the third day, the child reached the old woman's home. When he reached there, he told the old woman what he wanted. The old woman told the boy to go in the granary and get firewood for cooking. When the boy reached there, he found there legs of people and he was shocked. When the boy told the old woman, the old woman chased the boy and the boy went running. When the boy reached home, he told his father and mother what he saw.

The boy telling his father and mother a story.

Two days later, she sent the next boy and told him to use what is given to him well and don't talk anything which you find there. The boy went and reached the old woman and the old woman welcomed him and told him the same words he told his brother. The boy went and moved legs of people they cooked millet and they ate. After eating the old woman told the boy to go in the granary with a knife and she also gave him a sack of millet, sorhum and a lake and she told him that when the animals comes cut the tail of the big and long tail. When it reached night the animals came and started smelling the boy but the old woman made them to sleep.

At the midle of the night, the boy moved out slowly and cut down the tail and he ran. The animals ran after him. When they were near him he threw a sack of millet and when animals reached there they picked the millet and the boy continued running. When the finished they again ran after him. When they near him he threw a sack of sorhum and the animals picked. After picking they again ran after him. he again threw a sack of a lake and he stood on the stone. Then the animals said you will find when I am a beautiful girl you will marry me, you will find when I am a good cow you will buy me the the animals went home and the boy gave the tail and gave it to his father.

The boy taking the tail at home.

On year later his father got healed and they went to the market. When they reached the market, he found there a beautiful cow and told his father to buy it but his father refused. When they went back home, the boy went to fetch water and found their the beautiful girl and took her to be his wife. After one week the girl started turning into the other animal

The boy looked for the panga to kill the animals but he found that was his wife but never minded.
In the afternoon they went to fetch water. When they reached the wall, the girl turned into the animal and ran after the boy to eat him. He had told his mother that if the leaf of this tree falls down send my dogs for help. When the leaf fell down the mother opened for the dogs and ran to where their owner was calling them. The boy had climbed the tree and the animal wa down. The dogs came and ate the animal and the boy survived.

ANDREW

35. The Man Who Ate His Eye

MY LIFE AT HOME

Once upon a time when I was young, I lived with my cousin and parents. We used to go in the garden. A cow ran after me then my cousin caught me. The next day we went to town and we toured. My cousin bought me some biscuits. When I was nine years we went to Ibanda. My mother worked from Ibanda. We planted a big banana plantation. After sometime I went to school to study. I was in boarding. After the term had ended, we went back home.

KATATUMBA → P.1 P.2
ACADEMY

P.3 P.4

P.5 P.6

I am going to school to study.

The weather at home was cold. In the evenings we would put on sweaters. In the mornings sometimes there was coldness. After the holiday, I went to another school. I was a dayscholar. One day my best friend told me a story about a man who ate his eye.

She told me that there was once a man. One day an eagle came and informed the people of the village that there was a party in heaven.

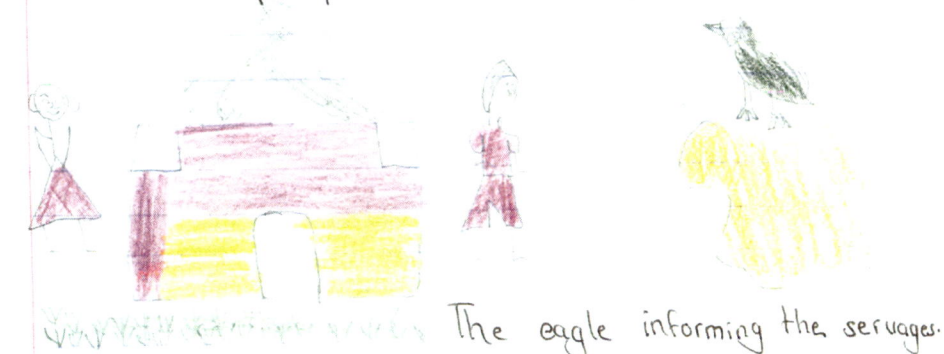

The eagle informing the servages.

The people wanted to attend the party. He told his father that he wanted to attend the party. His father never wanted him to attend the party. After three weeks, the servages saw many eagles coming. Oh! they wondered why the eagles had come. The leader of the eagles said that they had come to pick the people who wanted to attend the party.

"We are taking those who want to attend the party"

People seeing eagles.

So the man was the first to climb the eagle. So those who wanted to attend the party climbed other eagles. The eagles started flying up into heaven. When they reached heaven, the man was told that he was the one to cook. So the organisers of the party told each one to remove an eye. They put all the eyes in one big pot. The man was greedy and happy. So they told him to cook the eyes. He was greedy and happy. So they told him to cook the eyes. He started cooking the eyes. As he was cooking, he drank the soup.

People reached heaven and moved the eyes.

When the eyes got ready, he stole one of the eyes. So he went and informed the guests that the meal was ready. They told him to go and put the eyes in ten dishes. Everybody was happy. They told the guests to pick an eye and the last was the cook. Everybody picked and the cook never did his eye. So the people understood that he had stolen one eye. So the others put their eyes back. The eagles came back and took the guests back to their village. The father told his son to always respect his elders.

The guests pick their eyes from the dishes

The man going home.

That teaches us to respect our elders, sisters and parents. That was the end of the story she told me. After that we went to Entebbe National airport to receive my father. He had travelled to Kenya. My mother gave us evening tea and we started watching television. When it reached supper time, my cousin served food.

SARAH

36. The Sad King

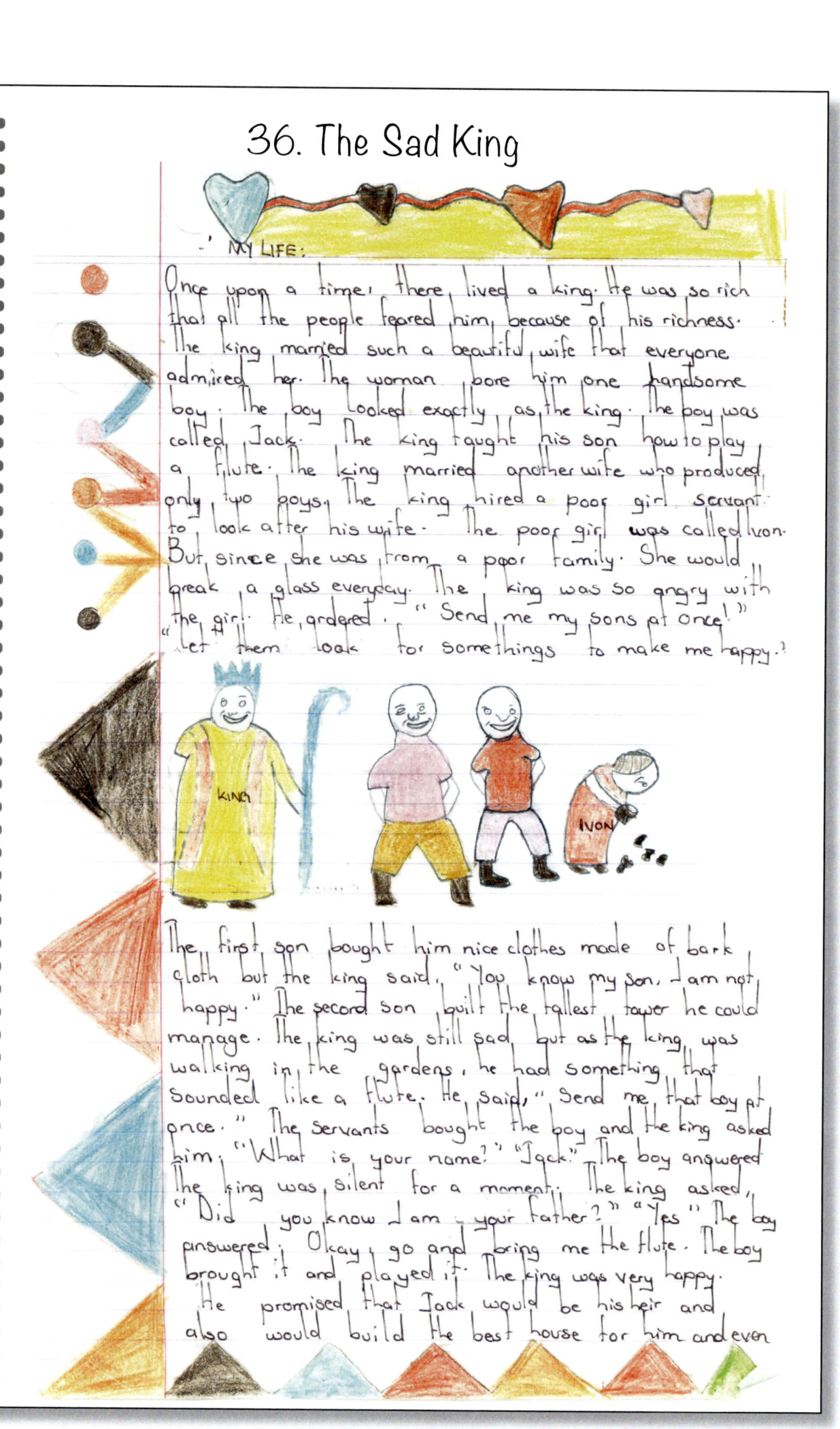

Once upon a time, there lived a king. He was so rich that all the people feared him because of his richness. The king married such a beautiful wife that everyone admired her. The woman bore him one handsome boy. The boy looked exactly as the king. The boy was called Jack. The king taught his son how to play a flute. The king married another wife who produced only two boys. The king hired a poor girl servant to look after his wife. The poor girl was called Ivon. But since she was from a poor family, she would break a glass everyday. The king was so angry with the girl. He ordered, "Send me my sons at once!" "Let them look for somethings to make me happy."

The first son bought him nice clothes made of bark cloth but the king said, "You know my son, I am not happy." The second son built the tallest tower he could manage. The king was still sad, but as the king was walking in the gardens, he had something that sounded like a flute. He said, "Send me that boy at once." The servants bought the boy and the king asked him, "What is your name?" "Jack." The boy answered. The king was silent for a moment. The king asked, "Did you know I am your father?" "Yes." The boy answered. "Okay, go and bring me the flute." The boy brought it and played it. The king was very happy. He promised that Jack would be his heir and also would build the best house for him and even take his mother as his wife for ever. They lived happily there after.

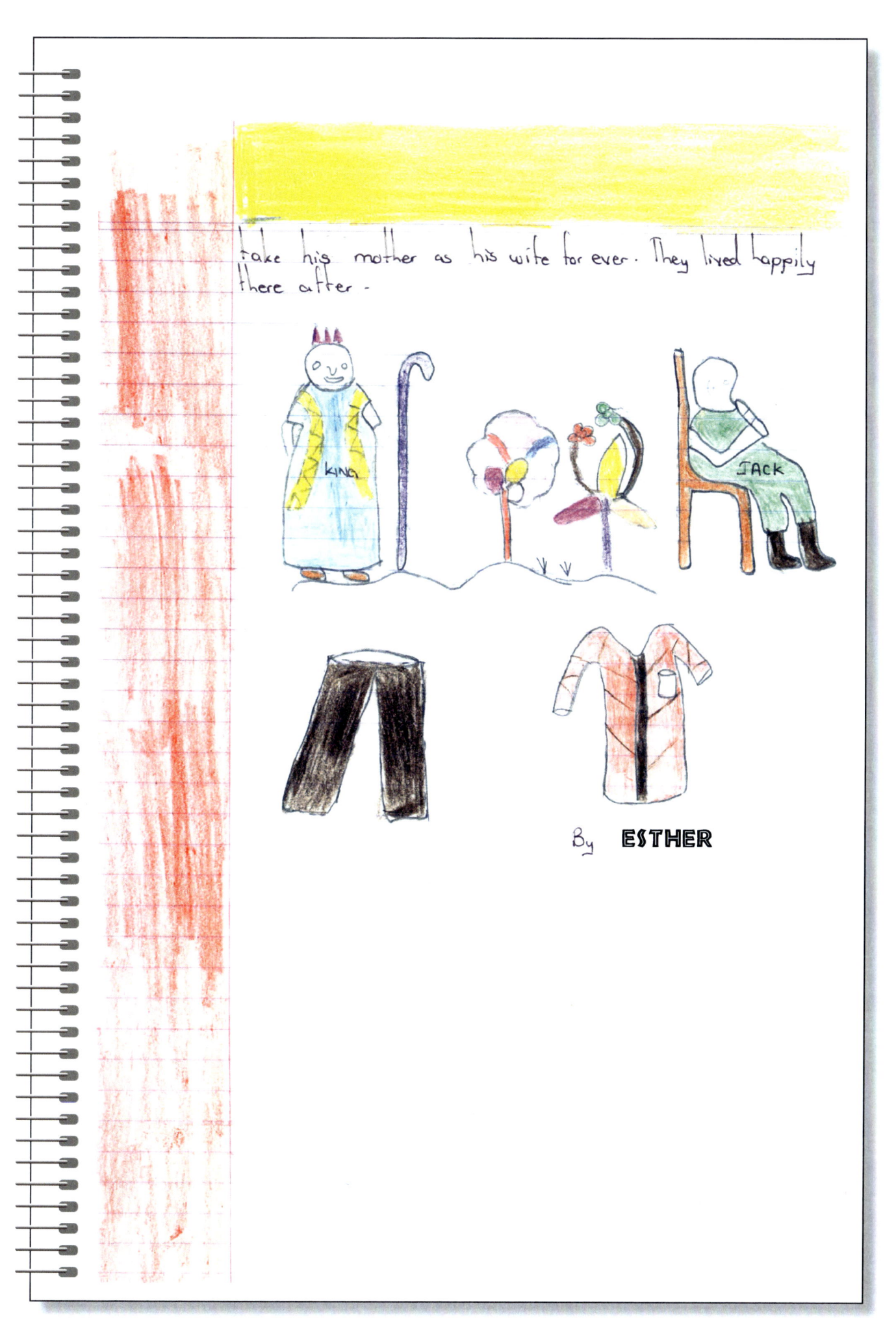

By ESTHER

37. Sisters - How To Behave

MY LIFE

Once uporn a time there lived a man in Kyarugendo village. He had one wife and tow daughters. One daughter was called Murungi and anodther was called Mubi

Murungi was beautiful, kind and helpful but mubi had bad behaviurs. She abused the poor and old people. She could laugh at the crippled ha ha ha did God create you when he was already tired?

Murungi always told her sister to get good behaviors but Mubi never listened. Her parents could tell her atleast mubi can't you fetch one jerrycun of water? Am I the one who told you to produce me

Mubi laughing at the crippled

One day the mother told them to collect firewood. Murungi said yes mummy we shall collect quickly Mubi said okay. but she told her sister Murungi since you are my younger sister you are going to first collect mine then you collect yours. Since Murungi was a good girl she accepted But when they reached home Mubi lied do you know mummy "I am the one who collected all this firewood. Murungi said no you told me to collect firewood because you are my elder sister" even keitesi was seeing us The mother said let's go to keitesi Mubi said no the mother said Murungi is the one who collected the firewood

Murungi   Mubi

The mother told mubi you have told me lies so I will not give you a gift Mubi cried and cried The mother said young children shouldn't tell lies

The mother gave Murungi a nice white dress and high shoes.
Murungi was like a pricess
Children I tell you listen what your Parents tell you don't be
selfish please be good children, kind and helpful

Murungi in a white dress her sheos

By PIA

38. Chris Finds A Baby

MY LIFE

Long time ago, there lived a boy and his mother. The boy was called Chris and his mother was called Santa. Chris was a very well behaved boy whose mother Santa was proud of.

One day, Santa sent Chris to the well to fetch some water. On his way, Chris met an abandoned baby along the road. Instead of continuing to the well, Chis picked the baby and took it home. "Where did you find that baby?" Santa asked. "I found the baby along the road," Chris answered. "Can I keep it, please?" Chris said. "Yes you can keep it but only if you promise to take care of it."

Chris finds a baby on the way.

Chris took care of the baby as he promised. Santa also helped him to take care of the baby as it grew. the baby was called Rebecca.

Chris takes care of the baby.

After ten years, Rebecca was twelve years she was very obedient to Santa and Chris. Santa and Chris liked Rebecca as their relative. Rebecca was so obedient that almost everybody liked her. Rebecca helped everybody in the village, whether young or old, sick or not and lazy or hardworking. Rebecca was respected by everybody and also trusted by everybody.

One day, Rebecca was going for a walk, she met a group of girls who were jealous of her, they were planning to beat her badly, they ran after her, she ran as fast as she could but it was already too late. The girls had already caught up with her, they beat her badly and ran away. She noticed their faces. So she went home and told Santa and Chris. Santa provided her with first aid. Santa and Chris were very sad. The next morning, Rebecca took Santa and Chris where the girls lived. "You girls are coming with us," Chris said. "No, you girls are not going anywhere with them," exclaimed one of the parents. "What have they done?" asked one of the parents. "So, you mean you don't know what your girls have done?" asked Santa. "Let's go," said Rebecca. Soon that day, they found out that the girls' parents were behind all this. So, they came with the police and arrested them.

Rebecca meets the girls.

The girls run after Rebecca.

The girls beat Rebecca.

Rebecca goes home.

After some days, the girls apologised to Rebecca and Rebecca forgave them. From then, they became best friends. When Rebecca grew old, she married a caring and kind man. She produced well behaved children, two boys and one girl. Before Chris left, he told Rebecca whatever happened. Rebecca narrated the story over the radio. The next day, her real mother came and told her what had happened. Rebecca forgave her mother and they lived happily ever after.

END BY **VITA**

39. How To Behave - A Lesson

MY LIFE.

One day, when I was at home with my mother, she told me a story about the badly behaved girl called Emily. Emily was a badly behaved girl who never liked helping her mother in doing domestic work, helping others when in problems and respecting the elders.

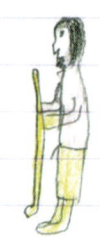

The girl is not giving respect to an old man.

One day when she was in her holidays after her s.4, she was looking for a job to get school fees for s.5. One day, one of her relatives came and told her that there was a vacancy in a certain shop. When Emily was going to talk to the woman about the job, she met her on her way to the shop carrying many things. She neither greeted her nor helped her. She just walked and reached the shop.

The girl neither helped the woman nor greeted her.

On reaching there, the woman was also behind her. She asked her what she wanted. Emily said that she wanted a job. The woman said that she can't give a job to a such merciless person. She went home annoyed

The woman asking Emily what she wanted

On reaching home, they asked her what the woman had told her. She never knew what to say so she lied that she was not there. She learnt to always help others.

Emily telling them what the woman had told her.

She was again called to work in another shop. She became merciful, she helped others when in problems and started to respect elders.

Emily respecting others by greeting.

When she went home, she told them about her change of behaviour. They were very happy. She got school fees for s.5 and completed her studies.

The people of at home happy after Emily telling them the change of her behaviour.

It was a very interesting story I had ever heard of in my life

PETRA

40. The Girl Who Sang

MY LIFE STORY.

I was born in Ibanda district of Uganda. When I was four years old, my mother told me to go by bus and visit my grandfather who lived in Kasese district. When I reached there my grandfather wecolmed me. After he had wecolmed me, I asked him to tell me the story of long ago. My grandfather told me the story of the "SLAVE GIRL".

Once a upon time there was a man called John. He had a wife called Mulungi. Mulungi produced one child called Jane. Jane knew how to sing very well but an accident happened, her mother had died. After her mother died, her father married another woman called Joan. Joan produced one daughter and one son. The stepmother of Jane liked her own children but not her. The father died. Two weeks after her father had died, the stepmother of Jane started treating Jane as a her slave, but because Jane knew how to sing the stepmother told her to teach her daughter how to sing. Jane taught her daughter how to sing and the stepmother became happy. Later at the home of James and Anna were getting married, they wanted a person to sing at their wedding. When the stepmother of Jane heard that, she ran to her home and told her daughter to be ready to sing at the wedding, she wore a black blouse of black, a red skirt of red and white shoes to sing at the wedding. When she reached there, she had got an accident. The people telephoned to her mother to come and take her child to the hospital, but people at the wedding wanted a person who knew how to sing. Fortunately they found Jane. They then asked her if she knew how to sing? She said yes, I know how to sing. They told her, what to wear to sing for them at the wedding. She wore a blouse of yellow, skirt of red and black shoes. She prepared to go and sing for James and Anna. Jane stood at the front to sing. She saw a handsome man Jane started singing, the handsome man heard her beautiful voice. After Jane singing people gave her gifts, and she was married to the handsome man.

MY GRANDFATHER STORY MADE MY LIFE, VERY HAPPY WHENEVER I REMEMBER IT.

MERCY

41. The Greedy Man

Once upon a time when I was born, I grew with my parents, sisters, brothers and my grandparents. After sometime, my mother died when I was still breastfeeding, then I stayed with the rest of my relatives.

One night when I was five years, our grandmother told us a story. Sometimes we used to do other activities like cooking, fetching water and many others.

One day, went to fetch water from the well and we saw a lion. I was very scared and started crying. My sister hid me and we later ran home. When we reached home, we told this to our grandmother. She comforted us and then she told us story which was about "A GREEDY MAN".

Grandmother telling us a story.

It went as follows; There was once a greedy man. He liked to eat every time. Once they said that the whole village was to attend a party. On that party, they had no meat to eat. So they decided to cut off each one's leg to act as meat. Then they asked, "Who is to cook?" The greedy man said that he wanted to cook and he was allowed.

When he was still cooking, he picked one leg and ate it. When the meat was ready, he took it for serving. When the greedy man was going to pick, they told him to let others pick first and then he picks last. All people got their legs. Unfortunately, there was no leg left for that man. They later realised that man had eaten his own leg and he went with one leg back home.

The greedy man stealing one leg.

people waiting for food

The greedy man going home with one leg

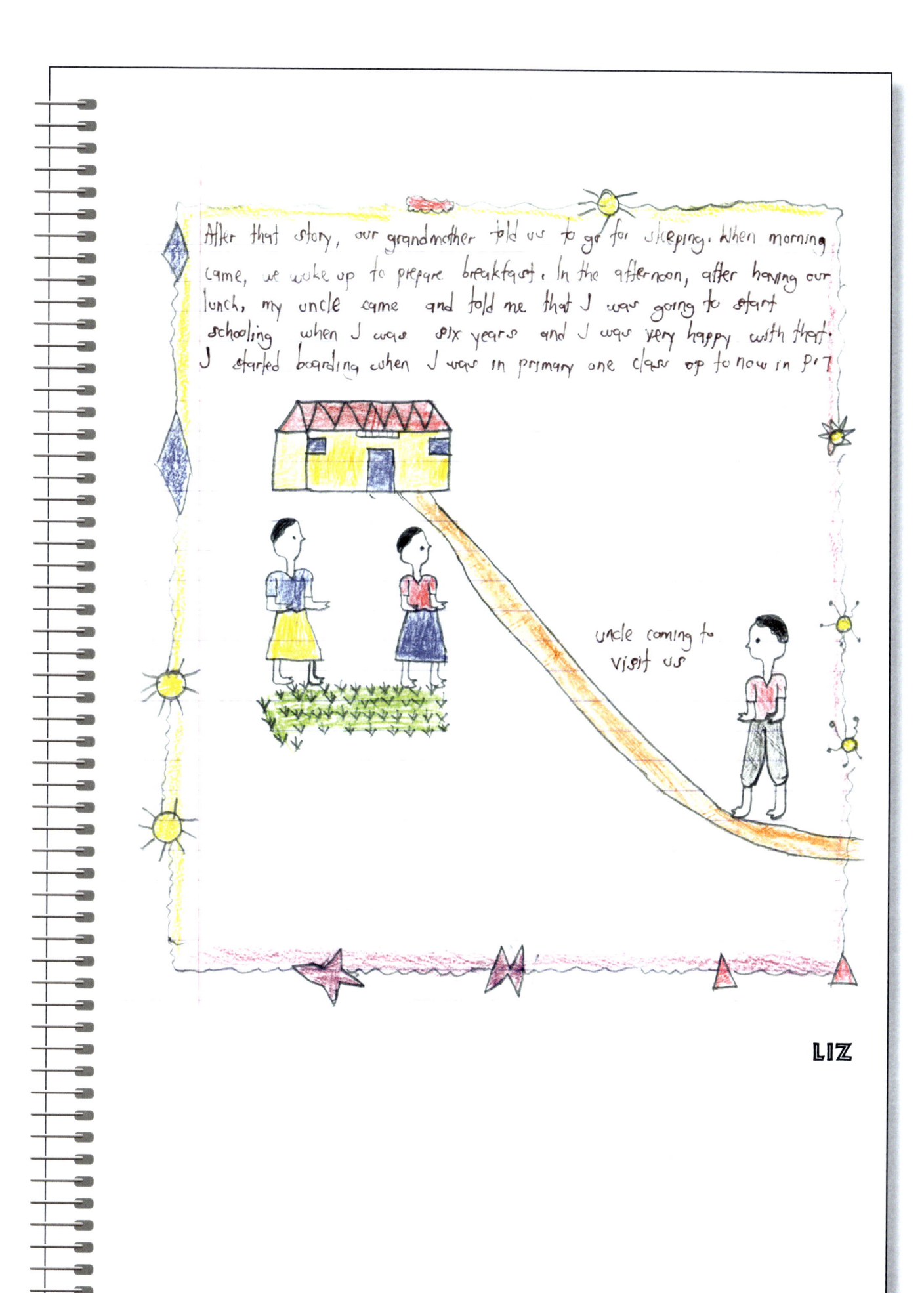

After that story, our grandmother told us to go for sleeping. When morning came, we woke up to prepare breakfast. In the afternoon, after having our lunch, my uncle came and told me that I was going to start schooling when I was six years and I was very happy with that. I started boarding when I was in primary one class up to now in P.7

uncle coming to visit us

LIZ

THE END